AF408929

An Islamic Approach to Time Travel

A Glimpse into How the Universe Works

ahmet yazici

Published by ahmet yazici, 2023.

While every precaution has been taken in the preparation of this book, the publisher assumes no responsibility for errors or omissions, or for damages resulting from the use of the information contained herein.

AN ISLAMIC APPROACH TO TIME TRAVEL

First edition. August 1, 2023.

Copyright © 2023 ahmet yazici.

ISBN: 979-8223316824

Written by ahmet yazici.

Table of Contents

To Muhammad Samir, Ahmad Shakir, Engin Demir,
Adem Kandemir, Bedirhan Kandemir, Erman Karaca,
Ahmet Yasin...

Introduction

Is time travel possible? Can man travel to the future or the past? Or can one travel to new dimensions by discovering new devices?

The most general definition of time travel is the ability to travel to any time period or location of your choosing based on your own decisions. While science anticipates the issue, Sufism has been quietly living this experience within itself for 1000s of years, counting the saints in previous nations.

In this material world, we are living a life of limited knowledge and experience, enslaved to worldliness. A century ago, technologies such as mobile phones, television, and the internet were considered to be quite far-fetched and impossible technologies and science fiction stories. So was a phenomenon like time travel. Although this has not been proven in terms of science, films made, books written, and articles published on this subject for years show that it is not impossible to travel in time. Scientific theories predict that time travel is possible when we approach and exceed the speed of light. Science will, of course, put forward new theories every day and will try to prove them by experimentation. Angels (when the distance and time they cover are calculated) must have a speed of at least 100s billion kilometers per second. And we do not have any information that the Angels have traveled in time. Perhaps speed is not a sufficient factor for time travel (or intergalactic journey). If we look on the bright side, perhaps there is no need to reach unimaginable speeds to time travel. Scientific developments may offer us more practical ways. Leaving the part of the issue that concerns science to science, I will deal with the Islamic and Sufi and logical aspects.

I built the time-traveling issue on two main ideas.

Firstly, I have mentioned in my previous works that the miracles of the prophets mentioned in the Qur'an are an incentive and a whip for mankind. If mankind works, they can realize miracles similar to the miracles in the prophets' stories through science and technique.

I have used the miracles of the saints as a reference to the issue. The miracles of the saints are very diverse. I have only written about the relevant ones.

Time traveling performed with scientific means will have common denominators with the miracles of the saints but will present many differences.

There may be those who do not believe in the miracles to be mentioned following pages, but each of them is a possible event. The stations and levels of each awliya differ from each other. Not all awliya can show the same miracles. Where appropriate, I preferred to generalize without mentioning the name of a saint.

People can realize the time traveling that the saints do as a miracle with the advancement of technology.

The second idea is that, in my opinion, shortly before the end of the world, some doors to the unseen worlds will be opened. Probably time traveling will also be possible to some extent.

We believe in the invisible and witness the visible. Hazrat Abdulkadir Geylani had watched Israfil in the sky while he was on the ground. His faith has risen to the degree of shuhud. We believe in angels; Abdulkadir Geylani is a witness (shuhud) to angels because he sees them. With the advancement of science and technology, we will believe in some unseen realms and beings at the degree of shuhud. Especially the jinn. Human beings could communicate with jinns and use them in certain areas.

And will the secret of the test not be broken?

If it were today, the secret of the test would be broken, but when it comes to the ummah of the apocalypse, things are different. You know that the apocalypse will break suddenly. So why do people get caught suddenly when the sun rises in the west? When the sun rises from the west, people will probably panic for a while, but scientific explanations will be made (they have been made and such an event is expected) and people will say that the apocalypse has nothing to do with religion. In the same way, if the doors of the realm of the unseen are opened, they will say that it has nothing to do with religion, it is the triumph of science.

We have expressed another one of the fitnah of the end times, which is to keep science and religion separate and to prefer science to religion. In fact, both are two rivers fed from the same source. The material universe, which science is interested in, is a book that came out of Allah's attribute of power, and the Qur'an is a book that came out of Allah's attribute of kalam.

I have made some quotations from Hazrat Badiuzzaman Said Nursi's Risale-i Nur. However, I preferred to transfer the meaning of most of the quotations instead of the full English translation. Anyway, reading the Risale-i Nur collection from translations does not give the flavor of reading it in Turkish. My advice to you is to learn enough Turkish to read the Risale-i Nur. Even if you do not fully understand what you read, your soul, heart, and conscience get their share. This is a recommendation to increase your benefit. You can also benefit from translations. I recommend two publishing houses for those who want to obtain both translated and Turkish-printed Risale-i Nur works. One is Envar Neşriyat and the other is Türkiye Diyanet Vakfı Publications.

Time and Space Travel as a Saint's Miracle

It is possible to see many examples in the Islamic literature that the awliya, who are profound in the spiritual field, traveled both in the past and in the future time during their spiritual journeys. In time travel theories, there are generally two ideas about traveling to the past. One is that you can go to the past and watch events but you cannot touch them. The other one means that if you can watch the past, you can touch it. This second view also gives rise to some paradoxes.

Traveling to the future time seems to be more possible. Therefore, I will not talk about traveling in the future time.

The saints can both watch and touch the past. There is no paradox. The main reason for this is that they do not act on behalf of their nafs/ego.

I would like to give an example of intervening in past events without giving the name of the awliya and the details of the event since I cannot find the source and I do not remember the event exactly. A great friend of Allah protected his mother from a malicious man before he was born. A man who followed the saint's mother in a deserted place intending to do evil heard a voice. (the incident may have happened in another way. This is how I remember it.) The man got scared and went away from there. One day, the awliya reminded his mother of this incident and informed her he was the one who drove the malicious man away.

A saint does not claim any miracles, he cannot say that the states that appear from him are miracles. Because it is permissible and possible that these states are a trick/ istidraj. The saints' miracles are true, but they are subject to Allah Almighty's will. The servant's will and power have no effect on it.

The miracles are usually narrated by witnesses. The saints traveling to past and future times do not have many witnesses. It is inferred from the books they have written that they have traveled in time.

Some awliya have foretold the events of the End Times and even the technologies of the End Times as if they had seen them 1000 years ago. There is no doubt that these saints spiritually see the events of past and future times. There is no definite information that they intervene in events and objects.

Now let's move on to time and space.

Assuming that there is no equivalent in English, I will share the Turkish versions of two famous concepts in Islamic literature: Bast-i time and tayy-i space.

Bast-i-time: Expansion and blessing of time. The state of having lived a long time in a short time.

- To have lived a very long time in a little time.

- To fit a long time into a small period of time and to be as if you have lived it.

Tayy-i space: To be able to appear in different places at once by transcending space. Skipping space; traveling a long distance in a short time with the help of Allah.

- Eliminating the place. The appearance of a person in various places at a time.

- Skipping, exceeding the dimension of space and distance.

- Traversing and crossing space and distance, traversing distances.

The scientific proof of Tayy-i space is quantum physics. The phenomenon of being in more than one place at the same time is one of the most fundamental concepts of quantum mechanics in modern physics. I have dealt with this subject in my work "Quantum to Ether." I will not mention Quantum mechanics in order not to deviate from our main subject.

To summarise; Bast-ı time means the expansion of time, seeing many things in a short time, and tayy-i space means transcending space, getting rid of the records of the concept of space, and being together in various places at once.

Allah can create space within space. He can also create time within time. The dream we experience every day is an example of Allah creating time within time.

Today's technology sends sound and images to many places at once through television, computers, tablets, and even the cell phones we carry in our pockets. No one is surprised by this. However, we find it difficult to comprehend how Belkis' throne was brought to Prophet Solomon (PBUH) in a very short time. If one day the teleportation of things takes place, we will not be surprised by it either, it will be quite ordinary.

Like the tide and ebb that occur in the seas, the issue of bast-i zaman (time) and tayy-i mekan (space) has become famous among the saints.

Tide and ebb are well-known and widely accepted sea phenomena. Similarly, bast al-time and tayy al-space are forms of miracles that are widely known and accepted among the awliya. When the body becomes subordinate to the soul and rises to the level of the soul, the time and space concepts cease to exist.

Imam al-Sha'rânî read the huge collection called Futuhat al-Makkiyah two and a half times in one day. Such facts should not be denied out of disgust. For there are many examples that bring such strange matters closer to confirmation. For example, in a dream, you see that a year passes in an hour and many works are seen. If you had read the Qur'an in that hour, you would have read several hatims. This state develops for the awliya in the state of jakaza (waking state). Time expands. The issue approaches the circle of the soul. The soul is already not bound by time. The works and actions of the awliya, whose spirit is superior to their corporeality, take place with the speed of the spirit.

As the tide and ebb occur in the sea with the permission of Allah with the effects of the moon and the sun, the states of bast al-time (expansion of time) and tayy al-space (shortening of space) occur with the manifestation of Shams-al Azal in awliya individuals who are like the sea, Oman.

When a person falls asleep, he is no longer bound by his physical body. A sleeping person does not require eyes to see, ears to hear, or feet to walk. In the dream, we do not use our eyes, ears, or feet that are connected to our bodies.

Every human being experiences a small example of bast-i time through dreams. They say that a dream lasts 4-6 seconds at most. There are also scientists who say a few minutes. Let's say two minutes. In a two-minute dream, we can live for years, get married, and have children. We can raise our children and marry them off. This is the expansion of time. Two minutes in external/temporal world, years in the sleep world. (Whether we spend an hour or a year in the dream world, the time in the visible world does not change.) We also experience an example of tayy-i space in our dreams. Suddenly, we are in a different place. Places, times, people, and events change in an instant. While we are talking to a person, before we even turn our face away from him, we see he has turned into another person. Or we find ourselves in a different place or time without realizing it.

What an ordinary person might encounter in a dream, the awliya can experience in real life. Tayy al-space allows them to go to the most remote locations, while bast al-time allows them to do tasks that would normally take years.

When the soul enters the dream world, it is free of the body and can do amazing things in a short period of time. These works are still taking place in this world. That is, in the temporal realm. However, still there has been a change in the realms. There has been a transition from the realm of jakaza (wakefulness) to the realm of nawm (sleep). When you enter another realm, the rules are different.

The saints can make others experience the miracles related to space and time. Let us give an example. A saint gives you trust and asks you to go to a place 10 hours away by plane and hand it over to someone. You want to ask about the plane ticket, passport, etc. He asks you to leave without asking. You decide to set off, thinking that there must be some wisdom. When you step out of the door and take a step, you see that you have arrived.

After completing the task, you come back again in one step. Or, if we don't want to completely ignore the reasons, this example fits well. There's a train leaving in 5 minutes. But the train station is half an hour away by car. He can take you to the station in one step.

***

Imam al-Suyūtī (rahimahullāh) said in his treatise al-Munjali fi Tatawwuri al-Walī: A person swore that Shaykh 'Abd al-Qadir al-Tashtūshī, the Wali servant of Allah, stayed with him one night, and if I am lying, let my wife be divorced, and another person swore to divorce his wife and said that Shaykh al-Tashtūshī himself stayed with him the same night, and he was asked which of these two people's divorce would be valid. So I sent a messenger to the aforementioned Shaykh 'Abd al-Qadir and asked him about this situation.

In reply, the sheikh said: "If even four people say that I stayed overnight with them on the same night, they are telling the truth."

So I gave a fatwa that the two men had not committed perjury (so their wives were not divorced).

The explanation of this according to Islamic law is as follows:

Some have claimed that it is not possible for a person to be in two different places at the same time, and that it is even impossible. The situation is not impossible as he thinks. Indeed, the famous and authoritative imams have said that it is permissible and possible. When this is possible, there is no such thing as a false oath. If a person swears by the existence of something that is possible, it is possible for him to be telling the truth, so it is not ruled that he has sworn falsely. Because talaq does not take place with doubt.

In a similar incident, Hazrat Aziz Mahmud Hudayi entered the spiritual path.

When Hudayi was a deputy qadi in Bursa, a woman came before him with a divorce case. She said that her husband did not go to Hajj even though he intended to go every year. She said that her husband had told her that he would divorce her if she did not go to Hajj again that year. However, she said that he had disappeared on the days of Arafah and Eid al-Adha and then reappeared and said that he had gone for Hajj, even though he had been absent until the day before Arafah. She said that she wanted to divorce her husband.

Her husband, who was with her, admitted that he did not leave his hometown until the day of 'Arafa. However, he claimed that he had gone on Hajj and that the friends he had met there could be asked to testify on their return, and that the reason for the talaq was not valid and divorce was not possible. The case was postponed by Mahmud Efendi, the deputy qadi, until the return of the pilgrims.

After the pilgrims returned, the testimony of the pilgrims proved that the wife's claim was true. Thereupon, Hazrat Hudayi announced the Sharia ruling that the talaq could not be valid.

Hazrat Hudayi announced his decree but secretly asked the person in question to find out how this had happened and what had taken place.

When Hazrat Hudayi said that he had attained bast al-time and tayy al-space through the spiritual guidance of a well-known person named Mehmed Dede, Hazrat Hudayi immediately ran to Mehmed Dede to ask for affiliation, but he said:

"Your fortune is not with us, it is with Hazrat Uftade, go and apply to him", so Hudayi went to Hazrat Uftade and affiliated with him.

***

Similar incidents are reported about Hazrat Badiuzzaman.

One day, when Badiuzzaman was in prison, the then Chief District Attorney of Eskisehir saw him in the bazaar. Amazed and astonished, he asked the prison warden, "Why did you take Badiuzzaman to the bazaar? I just saw him in the bazaar." The warden said, "No sir, Badiuzzaman is in prison, even in isolation. Look," he replies.

They see that Badiuzzaman is in his place. This marvelous incident becomes known in the courthouse. The judges say to each other, "We cannot comprehend this situation."

A case just like this happened when Badiuzzaman was in Denizli prison. The public saw him two or three times during the Fajr prayer in various mosques. The prosecutor heard. The prosecutor hears about it and says to the prison warden: "You took Badiuzzaman out to the mosque for the Fajr prayer". He made an investigation and found that Badiuzzaman was never taken out of prison. When he was in Eskisehir prison, one Friday, the prison warden was sitting with the clerk when he heard a voice: "Mr. Warden! Warden!" The warden looks. Badiuzzaman said in a loud voice: "I absolutely have to be at the White Mosque today. Warden: "Yes, Your Holiness," he replies. He thinks to himself: "I guess Hodja Effendi doesn't know that he is in prison and cannot go out," and retires to his room. At noon, he goes to Badiuzzaman's barracks, thinking that he would appease him and explain to him that he could not go to the White Mosque. He looks out of the ward window and sees that Badiuzzaman is not there! He immediately asks the gendarmerie, "He was inside, and the door is locked". He immediately rushes to the mosque. He sees Badiuzzaman praying ahead, in the first row, on the right side. At the end of the prayer, not seeing Badiuzzaman in his place, he immediately returned to the prison and was astonished to see Hazrat Badiuzzaman prostrating himself saying "Allahu akbar".

***

Somuncu Baba performed a similar miracle at the opening of the Ulu Cami (Great Mosque) in Bursa.

After the victory at Nigbolu, Yildirim Bayezid Khan started to build the Great Mosque in Bursa. During the construction of the mosque, Somuncu Baba provided the workers' need for bread. After the construction of the mosque was completed, it was announced that an opening ceremony would be held on a Friday. On that day, Sultan (Ottoman) Yildirim Bayezid Khan, his son-in-law, the great Islamic scholar and saint Seyyid Emir Sultan, Mullah Fenari, many Islamic scholars, and the people of Bursa filled the Great Mosque.

When Yıldırım Bayezid Khan assigned Emir Sultan to read the opening sermon of the mosque, Emir Sultan said, "My Sultan! It is not appropriate for us to read the sermon while the great scholar of the time is here. The person who is worthy of reading the opening sermon of this mosque is this person," and pointed to Somuncu Baba. Somuncu Baba, who meticulously avoided fame, walked toward the pulpit upon the order of the Sultan. When he came to Emir Sultan, he said, "O Emir, why did you do this and give me away?" He replied, "I did so because I could not see anyone ahead of you."

The congregation listened to these conversations in amazement and waited eagerly for Somuncu Baba's sermon. Somuncu Baba ascended the pulpit and delivered such a sermon that the people of Bursa had never heard such a sermon until then. Only then did the people of Bursa realize the greatness of Somuncu Baba. In the sermon, Somuncu Baba said: "There are some parts of the tafsir of Fatiha-i Sharif that some scholars cannot understand. Therefore, let us make a tafsir of this surah." He made seven kinds of tafsir of Surah Fatiha on twenty main sciences. He declared so many wise words that everyone was astonished. The first tafsir of Fatiha was understood by all the congregation. The second tafsir was understood by some of them, and the third tafsir was understood by very few. And nobody among the congregation understood the fourth and following ones. Even great scholars like Mullah Fenari.

After the Friday prayer, the whole community wanted to kiss Somuncu Baba's hand and receive his blessing. Unable to break this desire of the congregation, Hazrat stood at the door. Everyone who came out of the three doors of the Great Mosque was saying, "I am honored to kiss Somuncu Baba's hand." Somuncu Baba, again showing a miracle, made the community kiss his hand by being at all three doors at the same time with the permission of Allah. Somunca Baba left Bursa after his secret was revealed.

***

A great cholera epidemic broke out in Istanbul during the time of this luminous man. Although the experts fulfilled all the reasons, they could not prevent the epidemic in any way. Finally, they decided to knock on Yahya Efendi's door. Yahya Efendi was a person who did not leave his dervish lodge much at that time. They arrive at the dervish lodge in Beşiktaş and Yahya Efendi is asked to pray at Hagia Sophia on Laylat al-Qadr. Hearing that Yahya Efendi would pray at Hagia Sophia on Laylat al-Qadr Night, all the people of Istanbul flocked to Hagia Sophia. A congregation of about 60 thousand people filled the Hagia Sophia. At that time, there is someone in the first row who is not a saint but an ordinary person. This person has taken the first row by praying the Asr prayer in the first row. With the evening adhan, he broke his fast with dates and water, prayed the evening prayer, and waited for the tarawih prayer. He knew that if he left the first row, he would not be able to take the first row again, so he did not leave the row to renew his ablution. He performs tarawih with the wudhu of 'Asr. Just as Yahya Effendi began to pray, this man's stomach began to growl. The man said, "If I leave the mosque to satisfy my needs, I will never be able to sit in the first row again. He also worries that the prayer will be over by the time I arrive. "I wonder if Yahya Effendi is aware of my condition," he thinks to himself. A man next to him (a great saint who hears the man's supplication and what is going on inside him. Yahya Effendi also hears the man and delegates the task to the saint next to the man) hears him. "What's wrong, brother, are you in trouble?" he asks. Embarrassed and silent, the man explains the situation. The saint raises his arm and tells the man to pass the robe through his arm. The man enters through the sleeve of the robe and finds himself in a place where he can fulfill his need with the saint. The man fulfills his need there. The saint raises his left arm and tells the man to enter through the sleeve of his robe. The man enters through the sleeve of the robe and finds himself again in the same place in the first row. When they return, Yahya Effendi's prayer has not ended, on the contrary, it continues from the second the man left for his need. This miracle shows that Allah can create time within time for His servants and allow them to go to different places within that time.

***

There are various "time in time in space in space" themed miracles that are rumored to have emanated from Shaykh Abdulkadir Geylani. I will tell you about one of them.

In the time of Shaykh Abdulkadir Geylani, there was a man of knowledge. This person used to deny the spiritual sultanate of the shaykh. One Friday, he entered the shaykh's masjid for a conversation. But his main purpose was to tease the sheikh. After a while, the sheikh entered the masjid. The man asked the sheikh: "O sheikh, so to say, those who are murshid could turn time subject to them and could do things that could not be done for years. Is it correct?"

The Sheikh answers: "Allah gives the dervishes such strength that they can do the work that can be done in 10-15 years in a very short time."

The man objects and says he does not believe it.

And they gave the prayer rug to that person.

They said, "Please take this away!"

...

That person wanted to renew his ablution in the fountain.

As soon as his hands hit the water, he found himself in a marketplace and in front of a locksmith shop. He watched the locksmith work for a while. He found his work very pleasant and ingenious. He was envious and went into the shop and said, "Will you teach me this art as well?" He convinced the locksmith and began working as his apprentice. He worked as a locksmith for eight years. When his master died, he married his wife. They had two boys. One morning, he came to the locksmith shop. He lit the fire to begin his work. While he was going to put an iron on the stove, he suddenly finds himself in the fountain where he had made an ablution.

While he is performing ablution in the fountain, the sheikh's prayer rug is standing on the tree (he hung it on the tree before he started the ablution).

He makes ablution and runs after the sheikh. He makes ablution and runs after the sheikh. As the sheikh enters the door, he catches up with the sheikh. He lays the prayer rug in front of the sheikh. He wants to retreat, but the sheikh asks him to sit next to him. Together with the Sheikh, they prayed two rak'ahs.

Sheikh asks: "Are you still in denial?"

The man tells with amazement what happened to him. He cannot make sense of what he is going through. He asks if this is all a dream. And he states that his heart is still with his wife and children.

Sheikh asks: "Do you know how many years it has been since this situation happened?"

"It's been over 10 years if it's up to me."

"Can you practice the locksmithing you learned now?"

"Here my hands are witnesses. Of course, I can."

"Know well that this job is neither imagination nor a dream. It really happened."

After praying, they wrote a letter to that city and brought the man's wife and children.

There are three ways in which the scholars have evaluated the issue of a person being in more than one place at the same time:

1. It is explained by being in more than one place through the appearance of forms and shapes, as in the case of jinn and angels.

2. It is explained through the wrapping of the distance and the removal of the earth without being in more than one place. In this case, each of the seers sees the awliya in his own house even though he is in one place. However, Allah (S.W.T) rolls up the ground and removes the obstacles that prevent passage, so it is

thought that the saint is in two different places. This is the best interpretation of the hadith that says that on the morning of Isra when the Messenger of Allah (PBUH) was in Makkah and described the features of Bayt al-Maqdis to the Quraysh, Bayt al-Maqdis brought before his eyes.

3. It is explained by the size of the body of the saint. That is, his body grows large enough to fill the universe and can be seen from everywhere.

Ala'ad al-Din al-Qūnawī (rahimahullāh) says in his book al-I'lām bi Ilmāmi'l-Arwāh Ba'de'l-Mawt Ale'l-Ajsām: It is possible for Allah (S.W.T) to grant some of His servants the power to dispose of another body while they are still alive, even though they are still disposing of their own body. It has been said that Abdals are called 'abdal' because they appear in one place and then appear in other places in a similar form (similitude, simulation) instead of their original form.

Let's open a parenthesis here.

The realm of similitude is a bridge realm between the material realm and the spirit realm. This realm has taken qualities from both the material realm and the spirit realm. Compared to the material realm, the realm of similitude is a lighter and gentler realm. The realm of similitude is a realm close to the imagination.

In the state of sleep, since the human being's relationship with the material world is cut off, his other spiritual organs and emotions are in contact with the unseen worlds. And he wanders there. Depending on the progress of the heart and emotions, he sometimes encounters the manifestations of the preserved tablet and sometimes the samples of the letters of destiny. This is the truth of the dream. These manifestations and samples seen in the dream take on the exaggerated shapes and forms of the realm of similitude. This is why dreams need interpretation. Because something simple in the realm of reality can become very big and complicated in the realm of similitude. The discoveries of some saints, which seem far from the mind, are also due to this truth. Some saints have reported their discoveries as they saw them in the realm of similitude.

The soul travels and contemplates the realm of similitude through imagination. The windows that are closed to the material world through sleep open to the spiritual and similitude worlds. The soul also travels and contemplates those worlds through these windows.

Based on this information, it can be said that dream travel is easier for humanity than time travel. The issue of the realm of similitude is actually related to the reality of time.

Tamassul (similitude, simulation) is the appearance of a thing in another form while preserving its original identity. In the Qur'an, tamassul is described in Surah Maryam, verse 17, as follows: "She placed a screen (to screen herself) from them; then We sent her our angel, and he appeared before her as a man in all respects."

Tamassul is an act that is possible for jinn, angels, and awliya. The wife of a great saint looks into the room through the hole in the door. She sees that there are 40 of her husband in the room. In this way, the productivity expected from 40 people can be achieved by one person, and works that would not be possible to be written in a lifetime can be achieved. (Even if he consistently writes, without eating, drinking, or sleeping.)

Spirits take on a body and appear in various forms. A single soul becomes the controller of both its original and its simulated form at the same time. It takes on both forms and manages and disposes of both at the same time. The Spirit of Gabriel (PBUH) is the most well-known example. When Gabriel (PBUH) came to the Prophet (PBUH) in the form of Dihya (R.A), his original body (that great body that covered the horizon with its wings) was unchanged. Allaah created another form, and the spirit of Gabriel (PBUH) was in both forms at the same time. Israfil (PBUH) is also performing different tasks while waiting to blow the trumpet.

***

We cannot understand these truths by assuming that existence is only matter. Nor is it possible to understand these truths by accepting the limitations of time and space in the matter as indispensable. To understand the reality of being in many places at once, we must first understand the concept of luminosity, which science ignores.

The mindless materialist approach restricts existence to what can be subjected to laboratory experiments and measurements. However, accepting luminosity as a dimension of existence that transcends time and space will pave the way for the science of physics. Even physical laws, such as gravity, are luminous and exist everywhere even though they are nowhere.

There are basically two aspects of beings: luminosity (lightness) and density (solidity, heaviness, hardness, harshness, dullness, opacity, darkness). Material beings are actually a mixture — in varying proportions — of luminosity and density. Men and women are the same in terms of matter. Both are solid. However, women have been called the gentle sex because of their lenity, elegance, gentleness, and kindness. Therefore, when we witness men's unobtrusive and rude actions and words emanating from women, we do not approve of them and find them very repulsive. Such behavior is repugnant because it is incompatible with the attribute of womanhood, which has angelic grace. To make a joke, men are wood and women are flowers.

The human being is composed of a solid body and a luminous soul. As a physical being, the human body is subject to the laws of physics. Therefore, he cannot be in more than one place at a time.

The soul, as a luminous being, transcends time and space. It is not under the control of any physical law. As a result, it can be in multiple locations or even everywhere at once. However, because the human being is a whole with a soul and a body, the soul and body must work together. In this case, the dominant element will win. If a person is fat in the body but lean in spirit, that spirit will be imprisoned in that body (the spirit becomes almost dense), and density will prevail. The individual will even claim that he is only a body. However, if the person is spiritually developed but physically weak, the opposite will occur, and the person's body will acquire luminosity and the principles of lightness will prevail in the person rather than the laws of physics. This person will then be able to be in multiple places at once, subject to the laws of the soul as well as the body that has gained luminosity.

This could be described by comparing the body to a balloon and the soul to helium gas, which is seven times lighter than air and swiftly rises when released. If we let go of a balloon with very little helium gas, it will descend to the ground due to gravity. In other words, the light helium gas will follow the same rule as the solid balloon material. That is, an under-inflated helium balloon is like a solid object. However, if helium gas is pumped into the balloon and then released, the rising force in the helium gas will triumph over the falling force dominating the balloon, and the helium-filled solid balloon will rise towards the heavens. Just as the laws of spirituality and the spirit govern the body. The dominance of the soul over the body and the dominance of the body over the soul is different for everyone. To the extent that the body dominates the soul, man degrades and becomes a devil. To the extent that the soul dominates the body, man advances spiritually and becomes angelic.

When the human senses rise to the level of the soul, ready time expands.

The senses carried by human beings are divided into classes such as vegetable, animal, human, and angelic. The natural and animal senses belong to the worldly life. And they prevent man from being in many places or at many different times. If these feelings rise to the level of the soul, some of the virtues inherent in the soul are revealed. Otherwise, time and space will limit the human being and he will not be able to go beyond the time and place he is in.

Humanity begins with reason. Human beings are different from all animals in this respect. A person who does not use his intellect cannot reach the level of humanity and has animal attributes and character (scorpion, pig, monkey character, etc.). He looks human on the outside, but on the inside, he is an animal. A person who uses the blessing of reason properly will be blessed with great humanity, that is, Islam.

Attachment to matter and addiction to worldly pleasures are at an all-time high in our day, and it has become extremely difficult for the heart and soul to develop and triumph over corporeality. By following certain of Allah's laws (Sunnah of Allah), these senses may improve and the spirit can triumph over corporeality. These are advancement in faith and marifatullah (to know Allah) in faith, dhikr, eating little, sleeping little, talking little, contemplation, abstaining from sins, fulfilling the obligatory duties, and following the Sunnah to the letter...

The heart gains transparency and becomes a bright mirror to the world of truths through principles like dhikr, thought, and asceticism. As a result, some truths and many secrets are reflected in that heart.

An incident from the Risale-i Nur Collection that exemplifies this issue: 'At one time, being instructed by Ghawth al-A'zam, Shaykh Geylani (May his mystery be sanctified), was the only son of an aged and anxious woman. This esteemed lady had gone to her son's cell and seen that he had nothing to eat but a piece of dry, black bread. Her maternal compassion was aroused by his emaciated condition resulting from his asceticism. She felt sorry for him. Later she went to Ghawth al-A'zam in order to complain, and saw the Shaykh was tucking into roast chicken. Out of her concern, she declared: "O Master! My son is dying of hunger while you are eating chicken!" Whereupon Ghawth al-A'zam said to the chicken: "Rise up, with God's permission!" At this, the cooked chicken bones assembled and were thrown out of the dish as an entire live chicken. This has been related unanimously through many reliable and documented channels as a marvel of someone whose extraordinary wonder-working is world-famous. Ghawth al-A'zam said to her: "When your son reaches this level, then he too can eat chicken."

Thus, the meaning of Ghawth al-A'zam's words is this: whenever your son's spirit rules his body, and his heart rules the desires of his soul, and his reason rules his stomach, and he wants pleasure for the sake of offering thanks, then he may eat delicious things.'

Here is another incident that shows us the superiority of the pure heart of the awliya, whose ranks are high:

Once, while Imam Abu Hanifa was teaching his students, a person came and informed him that a ship that was carrying a large quantity of his merchandise had sunk. Imam Abu Hanifa lowered his gaze toward his heart, paused for a while, and said calmly: "Alhamdulillah." Then he continued to teach. After, the same person came again and said that the information was false. The ship was safe. Again, Imam Abu Hanifa looked towards his heart, waited for a while, and said calmly: "Alhamdulillah." He then continued the lesson. Later, he was asked about the wisdom of his act. Imam Abu Hanifa said: "When I heard the ship had sunk, I checked my heart to see if it was uneasy. Since I found it was unmoved, I said Alhamdulillah (Praise be to God). When I was informed that the news was false and that the ship was safe, I again checked my heart and again found it unmoved I said Alhamdulillah."

In conclusion;

Badiuzzaman's example of someone who missed last night's Laylat Al-Qadir summarizes what I have written so far (not an exact English translation, I have quoted it as a close meaning): "... It is to get rid of the material body, which is bound by time, and to rise spiritually through transcendence, and to see last night's Laylat al-Qadr as ready as it is today, together with the next day's Laylat al-Id. Because the soul is not bound by time. When the human senses rise to the level of the soul, that ready time expands; times that are past and future in relation to others are ready in relation to him. According to this representation, to pass to last night's Laylat al-Qadr is to ascend to the level of the soul and see the past as ready."

The people of truth who go behind time see the past and the future at the moment. For them, all time comprises a moment. Time is a moment for him. He is in the moment.

The Truth of Time

Muslim scholars have concluded that there are different types and characteristics of time-based on Quranic statements and terminology about time. Their classifications differ. They have, however, concentrated on two types of time: earthly time and metaphysical time.

Earthly time, also known as private time or physical time, is a time determined by the movement of bodies in space. It is used to measure human life and is valid in three ways: past, present, and future.

In earthly time, there is a phenomenon that arises from personal experience. Scholars have given different names to this phenomenon. These are psychological time, expanding time, and existential time. These expressions show how the influence of time varies from person to person. An hour in the waiting room is not the same as an hour at the amusement park.

It is not a mistake to claim that metaphysical time is above earth-based time. This sort of time is known in the literature as Pre-Creation Time, Eschatological Time, and Divine Time. When this time is compared to a circle, the time we know is a circle drawn inside this circle. This kind of time existed before the heavens and the earth were created, and it will continue to exist after they are destroyed. We are unable to measure such time. Because the unit of measurement for these is substantially different from earthly time. Metaphysical time includes the time of the Throne and the water, the time of the creation of the heavens and the earth, the time of the ascension of the angels and the Spirit (Gabriel), and the time of the Hereafter.

The angels and the Spirit ascend unto him in a Day the measure whereof is (as) fifty thousand years. (Al Maarij 70:4)

He rules (all) affairs from the heavens to the earth: in the end will (all affairs) go up to Him, on a Day, the space whereof will be (as) a thousand years of your reckoning. (As-Sajdah 32:5)

Metaphysical time and other time types are created by Almighty God, and evaluations of its reality and nature are found in the works of Muslim theologians, philosophers, Sufis, jurists, and historians. Al-Taftazani's Aqa'id al-Nasafi explains that time is defined for things that have a beginning, but God is beyond all measurements and limitations.

All kinds of time are for the created beings. Allah is free from time.

According to the Qur'an, the universe is divided into two parts: the seen universe (realm al-shuhud) and the unseen universe (realm al-ghayb). The division of the universe into realm al-ghayb (the unseen realm) and "realm al-shuhud" (the visible realm) is only for us. Nothing is unseen (ghayb) to Allah. Everything and every event was written before it entered the realm of existence. The beginning of everything and the events that will happen in the future are organized in the realm al-ghayb. This tablet is called the Imam of Mubin, which refers to an aspect of Allah's knowledge and command and is a book written by Divine Providence. These recorded events occur in the realm of the external and present times. The Almighty creates the events in the Book of Mubin, known as the "tablet of appearance and dissolution (lev-i mahv, Isbat)", which determines how everything, down to the particles, will act in due time.

"Imam of Mubin" is a title for a type of knowledge and command of the Divine, which looks to the unseen world rather than the world of the Shahada. It looks at the past and the future rather than the present."

"Book of Mubin", on the other hand, looks at the external world rather than the unseen world. That is, it looks at the present rather than the past and the future, and it is a title, a notebook, a book of the power and will of God rather than knowledge and command. If Imam of Mubin is the book of destiny; Book of Mubin is the book of power."

The Imam of Mubin looks at the result and purpose of the work, and the judgment is made accordingly. It is an unchanging, fixed, and eternally determined book of knowledge in terms of being related to the origin of everything and judging the end of events. The Book of Mubin, on the other hand, looks at the apparent, the observed, and the ready state of everything. It does not look at its reality, essence, and outcome. It is a kind of signboard for writing and erasing we call "Tablet of Appearance and Dissolution (lev-i mahv, Isbat)". Allah says in the Quran: "Allah doth blot out or confirm what He pleaseth: with Him is the Mother of the Book (13:39)."

Many of our commentators declare that one aspect of the Book of Mubin is the Holy Quran. According to one version, the Book of Mubin consists of the Qur'an. It contains everything, wet and dry.

So what is the reality of time? According to Badiuzzaman, the reality of what we call time, a mighty river flowing through the universe, is like the page and ink of power as it writes on the tablet of appearance and dissolution.

Islamic scholars have expressed various opinions about the Book of Mubin, Imam of Mubin, and Lawh al-Mahfuz (Preserved tablet). I wished to mention it to tie in with the topic of time travel. Suffice it to say that the Book of Mubin and the Imam of Mubin are the notebooks of Lawh al-Mahfuz.

Yes, Badiuzzaman Said Nursi compares time to a river. These creatures are constantly flowing in the river of time with the permission of God, they are sent from the realm of the unseen, they are clothed with a physical body in the realm of the external, and then they are regularly raining and descending to the realm of the unseen. And with the command of Rabb (rabbinical), they continuously come from the future, visit the present, stop by in passing pausing for a breath, and are poured into the past.

According to Badiuzzaman, the past and future belong to the realm of the Unseen, whereas the present belongs to the realm of Shuhud. From his statements, we can deduce the following. The future flows into the present tense, and after stopping here, it goes to the past tense. By situating the past and the future within a certain framework, the Qur'an uses both the present and the muzari tense for events that have happened, are happening, or will happen according to the human perspective (Muzari verb: a verb that expresses a work, a happening, or an action in the present, present continuous, and future tenses).

The Western view says that time moves in a linear, straight line. Badiuzzaman, on the other hand, states that time does not move in a straight line, but in a spiral circle. According to the Western perception of time, linear time, the river of time flows from the past to the future. In the linear perception of time, if we want to divide time, we can at most divide it at a single point. In this perception of time, we are constantly moving away from the past. There is no possibility of an intersection with other times. The Islamic perception of time, the circular perception of time, on the other hand, does not break our connection with the past. It creates new circles by constantly revolving spirally to the upper circles in parallel to the old circles. These new circles are not the same width. The circles of hours, days, seasons, and human life complete themselves and transfer themselves to the circle of the next hour, day, and season. Tomorrow it will be morning again. Today's morning will form a new circle at the beginning of tomorrow's morning, parallel to it (not a repeating circle, but an evolving circle), and it will be transferred to tomorrow's morning. This fall season will carry over to next year's fall season in the same way. When the circle is complete, we enter not into last year's fall season, but into a new parallel spiral circle at the beginning of the circle of last year's fall season. The circle of hours, days, seasons, and human lifespans add up to form the largest circle of time of six days (the creation of the universe in six days). When this single largest circle in six chapters is completed, it passes its judgment to the Hereafter. Contrary to the Western view, according to the spiral perception of time adopted by Islam, time does not actually disappear. The small circles are summed up and their judgments are transferred to larger circles. Seconds add up to minutes, minutes add up to hours, hours add up to days, days add up to months, months add up to years, and years add up to human lifespans. The circle of human life transfers its judgment to the largest circle of six days. When the largest circle of six days completes its circle, it transfers its judgment to the Hereafter, and thus to another realm. In linear time, time lags behind and disappears. In circular time, on the other hand, we see that the rule of time is transferred to wider circles. In this perception of time, we do not break away from the past, and when we come to the present, we find many points of intersection with the past.

The five times of prayer (6 times of prayer with Tahajjud) connect small circles of time with larger circles of time. Prayer times create divisions and intersections in spiral circles, opening a corridor of time and allowing us to travel. Prayer times are the joints or intersections of spiral time. I will add at the end of the book Badiuzzaman's views on the wisdom of establishing 5 fixed times of prayer. Badiuzzaman has expressed the intersections of prayer times in a wonderful way. You will also find Badiuzzaman's metaphor of the great clock in the same excerpt. Time is spiral, but those who cannot ascend spiritually cannot always go up to the upper circles by spinning in the same circle. It is the saints who experience this perception of time. We can experience the relativity of time according to the points where we divide time. In action movies, the movie ends quickly because there are too many divisions. But a psychological movie takes longer because there are fewer divisions and time is expanded. Each civilization has a different division of time. Modern man's time is very fragmented and flows fast. Islam wants us to divide time at the most accurate points, which are the times of prayer.

It is stated that the earth will be placed in heaven as a destination and will be open to visitors as a blessing from heaven. During this visit, it can be said that the events in the world will be watched live by traveling through time. We are also going to our past on the way to our future. I think we will realize this fact on the morning of the Hashir. I think that in the hereafter (heaven or hell) we will remember our memories in the world through the intersections in time.

Can Destiny be Changed by Time Travelling?

I have covered the subject of Lawh al-Mahfuz (Preserved Tablet) in the previous pages to link it to this topic.

The writing, the judgment, and the information on the Preserved Tablet never change.

Only the sub-tablets change. For example, on the sub-tablets, it is written that on such-and-such a day at such-and-such an hour, a flower pot will fall on a person's head due to the wind, and that person will be injured in the head. The angel concerned waits to fulfill this task. The servant approaches the place. At that time, a beggar asks for help. The servant gives him alms. Because the servant gives charity, Allah removes the trouble. Allah erases the writing on the sub-tablet that a flower pot will fall on the head of the such-and-such servant. The angel looks at the sub-tablet and sees that the writing has been erased. And the flower pot does not fall.

The writings on the sub-tablets are constantly being written and erased by scribe angels at God's command. However, the final state of affairs and events is written on the preserved tablet. It was already written on the preserved tablet that the flower pot would not fall on that slave's head. Allah knew that the servant would give charity and through that charity, He would remove the calamity from him. That is why He had written it on the preserved tablet. Likewise, prayer changes destiny. That is, the writings on the sub-tablets change with prayer.

The slave has a particular will. Therefore, he is responsible for his actions.

Let's say someone pushed a friend of ours last month. He hit his neck on a sharp point and suffered partial paralysis. Can we go back to the day of the incident and change the course of events and prevent our friend from becoming paralyzed? If we don't let the person who pushed our friend get any closer to our friend or if we intercept them at the last moment, will today change?

Let's answer this question like this. Is our friend paralyzed today? The answer is yes, he is partially paralyzed today, so we cannot go back in time and change the present.

So if our friend is paralyzed now, it is his destiny and we cannot change it. As I said, we have the will and we are responsible for our actions.

What would have happened if someone from the year 2010 time traveled and saw us at the scene of the tragic incident a month ago and prevented our friend from hitting his neck? Would today have changed?

Yes, it would have changed. Our friend would not have been partially paralyzed.

So every event happens once in the same time and space. If someone time travels and changes the course of events, we cannot realize that the course of events has changed. Our friend would not have been paralyzed, and we would never think of that bad incident. Maybe it was written in the sub-tablets that our friend would be paralyzed, but it was erased. We would not have known about it. However, the Awliya can see the sub-tablets to the extent that Allah permits.

Can we go back to before the first world war and change the course of events and prevent the war from starting?

No way. We cannot change anything written in history books.

Could a malevolent time traveler living in the 2100s go back in time and start the first world war?

Yes, he could. Because according to the history books, this war was fought. So this man is not changing the past. He is changing the course of events before they happen.

So, in some essentials, intervention in the past is no different from intervention in the present. If I am free to do an act of my own will today, I am also free to do some acts by traveling to the past. Whatever I want to do with my will, Allah creates that act. If someone built a time machine in the future and traveled to the past and intervened in the past, today we suffer the consequences of that intervened past. If we build a time machine today and go to the past and change the course of events, nothing will change today. More precisely, what we experience today will be the result of our past interventions. Because everything happens once. Allah creates what we choose.

Today I am free to shoot someone with a pistol. What happens to that man depends on whether I pull the trigger or not. So I don't know fate, I just use my will and pull the trigger or not. God creates whatever I choose. And He creates whatever will be the result of that action. Or I am driving a car and a child cuts in front of me. I am obliged to press the brake. I cannot know fate. The same rule applies to traveling to the past.

So won't someone who finds a time machine in 2100 go back to the past to change the past? In that case, how can every event happen only once?

The answer to this question is very general and answers many questions. The past, present and future are valid for us who are bound by time. Allah knew that a time machine would be built in 2100 and that we would go back to 1850. He creates events accordingly. He wrote it in that way on the preserved tablet. Therefore, no one can change the events known to have happened in the past by traveling back in time. In other words, Allah has written destiny knowing all interventions, all intersections, and conflicts.

Of course, we say all this assuming that time travel will be made in the 2100s.

Let us continue with the most famous paradox. Let's kill our grandmother so we'll never be born. That's not possible.

But what's to stop us from traveling back in time?

There are some people, good or bad, who are on a mission. They have always existed throughout history. For example, a nation is destined for trouble. Allah sends a cruel ruler to them. Many assassinations are organized against that cruel ruler and he never dies. Each time an unexpected event takes place at the last moment and that cruel person manages to survive. Allah does not allow that person to die. Allah may also send a good person and they will not succeed in killing him. When we want to kill our grandmother, there is always a mishap or an unexpected obstacle.

The other answer to this question is also one of the most important rules of time travel. There are writings in Destiny that cannot be changed. We can neither go back in time nor change them today. I am a Turk. Let me go back and change my kinship ties. That way I can be born Dutch and become richer. That is not possible. No one can change their lineage, their nationality. Or no one can change their sex.

And what will prevent this?

The obstacle we mentioned in the example of the grandmother also applies to this. We also mentioned the intersection points in spiral time perception. Perhaps these intersection points will not leave any room for paradoxes.

Can one travel back in time to save the grandmother's life, but not to kill her?

Yes, you can. If the grandmother's life is saved, we can exist today. We exist today. Therefore, the grandmother's life can be saved during our journey to the past.

I mentioned the ignorance of the people of the End Times. I stated that although they see some truths of faith, they will not believe. When a person intends to kill his grandmother when traveling in time, perhaps the beings belonging to the unseen world will understand his evil intention and prevent it. This man will still continue his denial. Because they will go too far in heedlessness.

What if the people of faith in the End Times see beings belonging to the unseen world?

This would be an incentive to strengthen their spiritual strength and an encouraging and morale-boosting gift in the difficult test conditions in the End Times.

If I could say one sentence about the grandmother paradox, it would be this:

If Allah wishes to activate this system (time traveling) to show it to His servants, He will activate it.

Grandmother paradoxes etc. are very extreme ideas. It is like a castle that has 100 doors, one of which is closed and 99 of which are open. We are trying to enter through the only closed door. We don't see the ninety-nine open doors.

***

What kind of time travel should we do so that there are no paradoxes?

Time travel is possible. There is no such thing that every possible thing will come true.

The most logical form of time travel is spiritual realisation. This way there is no room for any paradox.

Everything in the universe is recorded. In the future, people may be able to watch past events through a device. We talked about dreams. Dreams can be recorded. A person can enter and travel in the dream world while awake.

Hazrat Ibn Arabi says, "When I came to the ruined place, I heard the sounds of dhikr." Because everything is recorded. It means that before that ruined place was demolished, it was a dhikr assembly. It means that the dhikr there has penetrated and permeated the stone and soil. Ibn Arabi says, "The influence of people with spirituality permeates the places." When you enter an Ottoman period mosque in Istanbul, its spiritual atmosphere attracts you more. However, it does not affect the mosques of the Republican period. The people and spirits that permeate the Ottoman mosque are not the same as the people and spirits that permeate the Republican period. People whose frequency perception is open feel that energy in holy places. Some feel it, some hear voices, and some meet with the luminous figures of the past.

It is mentioned in Ibn Arabi's work: A friend of Allah enters the Nile River. The place where he comes out is not the place where he entered the river. He cannot find his own village or town. He has lived there for eight years, has married, and has three children. He enters the Nile River again. This time, the place where he comes out is the place where he first entered. He goes home and asks his wife how long he has been absent. His wife states that it has been 2–3 hours since he left home. He tells his wife that he has been away from home for eight years, that he's been married, and that he has three children. He investigates that village. He learns that there really is such a village. He brings his wife and three children. So, in three hours, he has lived eight years of life. Doesn't it bring to mind wormholes (even though it doesn't look much like a river)? Perhaps there are many more secrets in the universe but we cannot solve them.

In Conclusion;

In the end times, I am of the opinion that the subjects that the saints show as miracles will be obtained through scientific studies.

Hazrat Ibn Arabi states that all the awliya who will come until the Day of Judgment were shown to him. He even states that he can draw images of all of them with paper and a pen. Allah's knowledge is not later, it is eternal and everlasting. Everything has already happened in the knowledge of Allah. In the knowledge of Allah, the judgment is over, and we are in heaven or hell. (However, the fact that everything is in the knowledge of Allah and the fact that it will in due course move from the realm of knowledge to the realm of power are two different things.) We are talking about the future because time binds us. If Allah puts a servant behind time, the servant can see all past and future times.

Why Five Times Prayer?

Badiuzzaman's statements on the wisdom of establishing the prayer at five specific times (six times with the Tahajjud prayer):
" Just like the second-hand, minute-hand, hour-hand, and day-hand of a clock which tells the weeks, the alternations of day and night, which are like the seconds of this world—a vast clock of God Almighty— and the years which tell its minutes, and the stages of human life-span which tell the hours, and the epochs of the world's life-span which tell the days look to one another, are examples of one another, resemble one another, and recall one another. For example: The time for fajr (before sunrise) corresponds to spring's birth, the moment when sperm takes refuge in the mother's womb, and to the first of the six consecutive days during which the heavens and earth were created. It recalls how God disposes His Power and acts in such times and events.

The time for zuhr (just past midday) may be likened or corresponds to the middle of summer, the completion of adolescence, and to the period of humanity's creation in the world's lifetime. It also points to God's manifestations of mercy and profusion of blessings in those events and times. The time for asr (afternoon) resembles autumn, old age, and the happy time of the Last Prophet, upon him be peace and blessings. It calls to mind the Divine acts and the All-Merciful's favors in them. The time for maghrib (sunset) reminds us of many creatures' decline at the end of autumn and also of our own death. It thus forewarns us of the world's destruction at the Resurrection's beginning, teaches us how to understand the manifestation of God's Majesty, and wakes us from a deep sleep of neglect. The time for isha (nightfall) calls to mind the world of darkness veiling all daytime objects with its black shroud, and winter covering the dead earth's surface with its white shroud. It also brings to mind the remaining works of the dead being forgotten, and points to this testing arena's inevitable, complete decline. Thus 'isha proclaims the awesome acts of the All-Overwhelming One of Majesty.

Night reminds us of winter, the grave, the Intermediate World, and how much our spirit needs the All-Merciful's Mercy. The late-night tahajjud Prayer reminds and warns us of how necessary this Prayer's light will be in the grave's darkness. By recalling the True Bestower's infinite bounties granted during these revolutions, it proclaims how worthy He is of praise and thanks. The next morning points to the morning following the Resurrection. Just as morning follows night and spring comes after winter, so the morning of the Resurrection or "spring" follows the intermediate life. Each appointed Prayer time is the beginning of a vital turning point and a reminder of greater revolutions or turning points in the universe's life. Through the awesome daily disposals of the Eternally Besought One's Power, the Prayer times remind us of the Divine Power's miracles and the Divine Mercy's gifts regardless of time or place. So the Prescribed Prayers, which are an innate duty, the basis of worship, and an unquestionable obligation, are most appropriate and fitted for these times."

"By nature we are weak, yet everything involves, affects, and saddens us. We have no power, yet are afflicted by calamities and enemies. We are extremely poor, yet have many needs. We are indolent and incapable, yet the burden of life is very heavy. Being human, we are connected with the rest of the world, yet what we love and are familiar with disappears, and the resulting grief causes us pain. Our mentality and senses inspire us toward glorious objectives and eternal gains, but we are unable, impatient, powerless, and have only a short lifetime. Given all of this, it will self-evidently be understood how essential a support for human spirit it is to present a petition through Prayer and supplication to the Court of an All-Powerful One of Majesty, an All-Compassionate One of Grace, at the time of fajr, and to seek help and success from Him. Such support is direly necessary to bear and endure the troubles and burdens waiting for us during daytime. Zuhr (noon) is the period of time when the day is at its zenith, and starts to move forward to complete its course. People take a break from their activities. The spirit needs a pause from the heedlessness and insensibility caused by hard work, and Divine bounties are fully manifest. So, praying at this time is good, necessary, agreeable, and proper. This Prayer gives relief from the pressures of daily life and heedlessness. We stand humbly in the presence of the Real Bestower of blessings, express gratitude, and pray for His help. We bow to demonstrate our helplessness before His Glory and Might, and prostrate to proclaim our wonder, love, and humility before His everlasting Perfection and matchless Grace.

Asr (afternoon) resembles and recalls the sad season of autumn, the mournful state of old age, and the distressing period at the end of time. The day's tasks are brought toward completion, and the Divine bounties received that day (e.g., health, safety, and good service in His way) have accumulated to form a great total. It is also the time when the sun fades away, proving that everything is impermanent. We, who long for eternity, are created for it and show reverence for favors received, also are saddened by separations. So we stand up, perform wudu' (ablution), and pray. Thus praying 'asr is an exalted duty, an appropriate service, a reasonable way of paying a debt of gratitude, and an agreeable pleasure. We acquire peace of mind and find true consolation and ease of spirit by supplicating at the Eternal Court of the Everlasting, the Eternally Self-Subsistent One, and seeking refuge in His infinite Mercy, offering thanks and praise for His endless bounties, bowing humbly before His Lordship's Might and Glory, and prostrating humbly before His Eternal Divinity. Evening reminds us of winter's beginning, the sad fare wells of elegant summer and autumn creatures, and our sorrowful separation from loved ones through death. It also recalls the time when the lamp of the earth— the sun—will be extinguished, and the earth's inhabitants will emigrate to the other world following this one's destruction. It is a severe warning for those who adore transient, ephemeral beloveds, each of whom will die. By its nature, the human spirit longs for an Eternal Beauty. During the evening Prayer, it turns toward the Eternal Being, Who does all these mighty works and commands huge heavenly bodies. It refuses to rely on anything finite and, standing in the presence of the Everlasting One, cries Allahu akbar (God is the All-Great). Then, by saying Al-hamdu lillah, we praise Him in awareness of His faultless Perfection, matchless Beauty and Grace, and infinite Mercy. Afterwards, by declaring: You alone do we worship, and from You alone do We seek help (1:5), we offer our worship of, and seek help from, His unassisted Lordship, un-partnered Divinity, and unshared Sovereignty. Bowing before His infinite Greatness, limitless Power, and perfect Honor and Glory, we demonstrate, with the rest of creation, our weakness and helplessness, humility and poverty by saying: "All-Glorified is my Lord, the All-Supreme." Prostrating in awareness of the undying Beauty and Grace of His Essence, His unchanging sacred Attributes, and His constant everlasting Perfection, we proclaim, through detachment from all other than Him, our love and servant-hood in wonder and self-abasement. Finding an All-Beautiful Permanent, an All-Compassionate Eternal One to Whom we say: "All-Glorified is my Lord, the All-Exalted," we declare our All-Exalted Lord free of any decline or fault. Then we sit reverently and offer all creatures' praises and glorifications to the Eternal, All-Powerful, and All-Majestic One. We also ask God to bestow peace and blessings on His holy Messenger in order to renew our allegiance to him, proclaim our obedience to His commands, and renew and strengthen our belief. By viewing the universe's wise order, we testify to the Creator's Oneness and Muhammad's Messengership, herald of the sovereignty of God's Lordship, proclaimer of what pleases Him, and interpreter of the Book of the Universe's signs or verses. Given this, how can we be truly human if we do not realize what an agreeable duty, a valuable and pleasurable service, a fine and beautiful worship, a serious matter, a significant conversation with the Creator, and a source of permanent happiness in this transient guest-house it is to perform the evening Prayer? The time of 'isha (nightfall), when night covers the earth, reminds us of the mighty disposals of the All-Majestic Powerful One's Lordship as the Changer of Night and Day. It calls to our mind the Divine activities of the All-Wise One of Perfection as the Subduer of the sun and the moon, observed in His turning the white page of day into the black page of night, and in His changing summer's beautifully colored script into winter's frigid white page. It recalls His acts as the Creator of life and death in sending the dead entity's remaining works to another world. It reminds us of the Creator of the heavens and earth's majestic control and graceful manifestations in the total destruction of this narrow, mortal, and lowly world and the unfolding of the broad, eternal, and majestic world of the Hereafter. It also warns that only the One Who so easily turns day into night, winter into summer, and this world into the other world can be the universe's Owner and true Master and is alone worthy to be worshipped and truly loved. At nightfall our spirits, infinitely helpless and weak, infinitely poor and needy, tossed to and fro by circumstances and whirling onward into a dark and unknown future, perform the isha Prayer. In a manner recalling Abraham's proclamation, I love not those that set (6:76), we seek refuge at the Court of the All-Living, the Ever-Worshipped, the Eternal Beloved One. From our transient life in this dark, fleeting world and dark future, we beseech the Enduring, All-Permanent One. For a moment of everlasting conversation, a few seconds of immortal life, we seek the All-Merciful and Compassionate's favors. We ask for the light of His guidance that will illuminate our world and our future, and bind up the pain from the decline of all creatures and friends. We forget the world, which has left us for the night, and pour out our heart's grief at the Court of Mercy. Before death-like sleep comes, after which anything can happen, we perform our "last" duty of worship. To close our day's activities on a favorable note, we pray and enter the presence of the Eternal Beloved and Worshipped One rather than that of the mortal ones we loved all day; the presence of the All-Powerful and Munificent One rather than that of the impotent creatures from which we begged all day; the presence of All-Compassionate Protector in the hope of being saved from the evil of the harmful creatures before which we trembled all day. We start the Prayer with Suratu'l-Fatiha, thus extolling and praising the Lord of the worlds, Perfect and Self-Sufficient, Compassionate and All¬Munificent, instead of flattering and feeling indebted to flawed, needy creatures. We move on to *You alone do We worship* (1:5). That is, despite our insignificance and being alone, through our connection with the Owner of the Day of Judgment, the Eternal Sovereign, we attain the status of an indulged guest and important officer in the universe. By saying *You alone do we worship and from You alone do we seek help* (1:5), we offer Him the worship of the huge congregation of all creatures and seek His assistance for them. Saying *Guide us to the Straight Path* (1: 6), we ask to be guided to the radiant, straight path leading to the eternal happiness. Saying *God is the All-Great*, we bow down and contemplate the Grandeur of the All-Majestic One. Like the plants and animals, that have now gone to sleep, the hidden suns and waking stars are like soldiers subject to His command, and His lamps and servants in this guesthouse of the world. We think of all creatures' universal prostration. That is, like the creatures that sleep at night, when all creation living in a certain year or age is discharged from the duty of worship by the command of "Be!" and it is like a well-ordered army of obedient soldiers, and is sent to the World of the Unseen, it prostrates on the rug of death in perfect orderliness saying, "God is the All-Great." They are resurrected in the spring by an arousing, life-giving trumpet-blast from the command of Be! and it is, and rise up to serve their Master. Insignificant humanity makes the same declaration in the presence of the All-Merciful One of Perfection, the All-Compassionate One of Grace, in wonder-struck love, eternity-tinged humility, and dignified self-effacement. We then prostrate and achieve a sort of Ascension.

Thus each Prescribed Prayer time points to a mighty revolution, is a sign to the Lord's tremendous activity, and a token of the universal Divine bounties. And so this matter is a result of perfect wisdom."

Don't miss out!

Visit the website below and you can sign up to receive emails whenever ahmet yazici publishes a new book. There's no charge and no obligation.

https://books2read.com/r/B-A-XNWH-KUZHC

BOOKS2READ

Connecting independent readers to independent writers.

Did you love *An Islamic Approach to Time Travel*? Then you should read *Big Crunch: Invisible Apocalyptic Machines*[1] by ahmet yazici!

[2]

The Hour is near.

The countdown to the apocalypse has begun.

It's like a ticking time bomb with ten seconds to go off. That's why we experience the truth that time speeds up when the apocalypse approaches.

---

1. https://books2read.com/u/47gZRg

2. https://books2read.com/u/47gZRg

From time to time, different fields of the scientific world make statements such as, "A thousand years later, our earth will be in this situation; 10 million years later, the sun will be like this; this country will be in this situation, etc." What if I told you that the world doesn't have a life span of 200 years?

We are about to count down to the apocalypse according to universe time.

The Prophet (PBUH) said, "The lifespan of my Ummah will not extend past 1500 years."

In this book, I attempted to describe the apocalyptic scenes described in the Qur'an and hadiths using modern astronomical discoveries and predictions (e.g., black holes, the Big Crunch...). My primary goal was to describe the apocalypse in terms of science and religion. The resulting work, however, is primarily about the secrets of the universe and the miracles of the Quran... I am confident that you will discover previously unknown secrets about the apocalypse and the universe.

I'm sure the scientific truths revealed by the Qur'an and the prophet (PBUH) fourteen centuries ago astounded you. Your astonishment will grow even stronger as you read this book.

How will the apocalypse break out? What are the possible apocalyptic scenarios with a scientific and heavenly approach?

Also by ahmet yazici

A Glimpse into How the Universe Works
Big Crunch: Invisible Apocalyptic Machines
An Islamic Approach to Time Travel

A Glimpse into the Unseen Realms
Unmaterial Molds
How to Understand the Soul: Spirit or Brain?
How Can Soothsayers Predict the Future?

End Times, Rise of Antichrist (Dajjal), and Golden Age
The Return of Jesus: Conquest of Rome
Armies of the Heavens: Divine Help in Wars

Standalone
Can God Create a Rock He Cannot Lift?: Omnipotence
Paradox

Wouldn't Eternal Life in Paradise Be Boring?: Life in Heaven
Do Humans and Apes Have the Same Ancestors?: Evolution
and Creation in Light of Striking Similarities
Do All Uncovered Women Go to Hell?
Is Coronavirus a Divine Warning?
Is the Quran the Word of God?
Who Created the Mobile Phone?
Why Did Islamic Countries Lag Behind?: Is Islam Not the
Right Religion?

About the Author

Ahmet Yazici lives in Turkey with his parents and brother. He likes to write non-fiction Islamic works that prove the truths of faith in a rational way and fiction works (primarily fantasy fiction).